Poems on
Shanghai Sun Island

Edited by Wong Yoon Wah and Tan Hong Khoon

上海太陽島詩選

王潤華　陳逢坤　編

文　史　哲　詩　叢
文史哲出版社印行

Table of Contents

Introduction:The Legend of Shanghai Sun Island ·············· 4
1.For My Cousin Cheqi ·············· 8
2.Poem on Wu Valley ·············· 10
3.Mao River ·············· 12
4.The River in Huating Valley ·············· 14
5.The River in Huating Valley ·············· 16
6.The River in Huating Valley ·············· 18
7.The Mao Pagoda ·············· 20
8.Mao River ·············· 22
9.The River in Huating Valley ·············· 24
10.Mao River ·············· 26
11.Ascending Mao Pagoda ·············· 28
12.The Mao Lake ·············· 30
13.An Account of Sailing to Mao River in Autumn ·········· 32
14.Sailing on the Mao River ·············· 34
15.On Lake Mao ·············· 36
16.Crossing the Mao River ·············· 38
17.Pagoda Garden of Fu Tian Temple ·············· 40
18.Lake Mao ·············· 42
19.Crossing the Mao River at night ·············· 44
20.Passing by the Mao River ·············· 46
21.The Travelogue of Xu Xiake ·············· 48
22.Looking at the Nine Peaks from Mao River ·············· 50
23.Climbing Up Mao Pagoda ·············· 52
24.After Visiting Mao Pagoda ·············· 54
25.Climbing Up Mao Pagoda ·············· 56
26.Crossing the Mao River ·············· 58
27.Written for the Painting "Sailing on River
   Mao in Autumn" ·············· 60
28.Written for the Painting "Sailing on the
   Mao River in Autumn" ·············· 62
29.Written for the Painting "Sailing on the
   Mao River in Autumn" ·············· 64
30.Written for the Painting "Sailing on the
   Mao River in Autumn" ·············· 66

目　次

編序者：從泖文化到現代文化的上海太陽島 ……………………… 5
1　贈從兄車騎 ……………………………………………………… 9
2　吳中即事 ………………………………………………………… 11
3　三泖 ……………………………………………………………… 13
4　華亭谷 …………………………………………………………… 15
5　華亭谷依韻和唐彥猷華亭十詠 ………………………………… 17
6　華亭谷次韻唐彥猷華亭十詠 …………………………………… 19
7　泖塔 ……………………………………………………………… 21
8　泖湖 ……………………………………………………………… 23
9　華亭谷追和唐彥猷華亭十詠 …………………………………… 25
10　泖湖 …………………………………………………………… 27
11　登泖詞 ………………………………………………………… 29
12　泖湖 …………………………………………………………… 31
13　秋日泛泖記 …………………………………………………… 33
14　泛泖 …………………………………………………………… 35
15　泛泖 …………………………………………………………… 37
16　渡泖 …………………………………………………………… 39
17　福田寺塔園記 ………………………………………………… 41
18　泖上 …………………………………………………………… 43
19　月夜遊泖湖 …………………………………………………… 45
20　泖上 …………………………………………………………… 47
21　徐霞客遊記 …………………………………………………… 49
22　泛泖遙望九峰 ………………………………………………… 51
23　登泖塔 ………………………………………………………… 53
24　遊泖塔次日抵昆山訪旅庵大師 ……………………………… 55
25　登泖塔 ………………………………………………………… 57
26　渡泖 …………………………………………………………… 59
27　題〈泖湖秋泛圖〉 …………………………………………… 61
28　題〈泖湖秋泛圖〉 …………………………………………… 63
29　題〈泖湖秋泛圖〉 …………………………………………… 65
30　題〈泖湖秋泛圖〉 …………………………………………… 67

Introduction:

The Legend of Shanghai Sun Island

Located in the middle of Huangpu River, the Shanghai SunIsland (www.sunislandclub.com) is shaped like a weaver's shuttle. The island is 160 hectares in area, 4,000 meters in length and 700 meters in width. It takes 40 minutes to an hour to reach the island by road from the city center of Shanghai.

Prime Group International of Singapore developed Sun Island into an integrated resort hotel and international golf club. In 1997, it was rated as a 5-star integrated resort by US timeshare giant Interval International. The island is reminiscent of Singapore, which is also an island in the sun, and this was one of the reasons that Mr Tan Hong Khoon, Chairman of Prime Group International, acquired it for redevelopment.

編者序

從泖文化到現代文化的上海太陽島

　　太陽島高爾夫溫泉度假酒店（簡稱太陽島 www.sunislandclub.com.）坐落於上海市後花園 —— 青浦區朱家角古鎮境內，位於黃浦江上游泖河之中，距市中心 45 公里，沿滬青平高速公路只需 40 分鐘就可抵達。歷史記載，島在唐代開始就有人居住，太陽島原名泖島，位於黃浦江上游泖河與太浦河交匯處的泖島上，泖河與澱山湖相通，太浦河又與太湖相連。島的四周連接泖河、太浦河和澱山湖、黃浦江、太湖流域接軌，是三大水域來往船隻的重要地標。

　　新加坡國際元立集團投資 2 億美金開發，1997 年被上海市建設委員會評爲上海十大旅遊景點。1997 年被 Interval International 國際組織評爲五星級度假村。2002 年被國家旅遊局評爲 4A 級旅遊景點。整個島嶼面積 2400 畝地，東西最寬 700 米，南北長 4 公里，繞島一周 10 公里。

　　太陽島形似梭子，河水川流不息，宛如在爲歷史織布、爲文明積澱成型。其間經歷了春秋戰國、兩漢盛唐…，商旅墨客在此雲集。許多名人，例如：王安石、

The original name of Sun Island is "Mao Island"; it was the mecca of cultural activities for businessmen, government officials, poets, artists and Buddhist monks in ancient times. The 1200-year-old Mao Pagoda standing on the island is a symbol of the enduring ancient Chinese culture. It attracted poets, writers and painters such as Wang Anshi, Xu Xiake, Zhu Xi, Dong Qichang, Zhao Mengfu and Lin Zexu who produced an enormous output of poems, prose, travelogues and paintings from the second century. The present collection, based on the tome entitled The Pictures of Sailing in Autumn Mao River, and edited by Xie Tianxiang, contains only some of the representative works.

The current volume consists of 30 pieces of poems and prose written by Chinese writers who visited Sun-Island over a period of 1200 years. These poems constitute the most vivid record of the natural and cultural landscape of Mao River and its island, past and present. They are extraordinary works of art and supreme expressions of the innermost thoughts and feelings of many great literary figures of China since the 6th century.

Wong Yoon Wah
Tan Hong Khoon

朱熹、趙孟頫、董其昌、林則徐，都在島上留下歷史的足跡與文化遺產。唐乾符年間，有僧人如海在湖中築台基建洇塔於上，並鑿井建亭，名澄照塔院。五層磚木結構的洇塔無疑是這片沉睡千年的處女地上的最好的見證物，建於唐代，有 1200 年的歷史，是太陽島的守護神，也是國家重點文物保護單位，是中國僅存五座古燈塔之一。

　　根據現存的資料，從晉朝以來，洇河與洇島歷代引發了文人墨客大量的詩詞、散文與繪畫，目前最完整的手存在謝天祥編輯的《洇河秋泛圖》（上海：學林出版社，1995）。本選集根據《洇河秋泛圖》精選了三十篇歷代命名家作品（27 首詩，三篇散文/遊記），僅此向編者及出版社致謝。我 2009 年 1 月冬天初訪太陽島，陳島主親自帶我們導覽太陽島，簡直從古代神游到現代，回到他的老總辦公室，眺望遠處的高爾夫球廠，他說曾經看見水池中有兩個夕陽，然後送給我唯一的《洇河秋泛圖》，為了讓這些歷代的風景視野走進國際，我們當時便計劃將其中一些名篇翻譯成英文，讓世人分享唐代陸龜蒙與明代徐霞客的經驗：

　　　　雲藏野寺分金剎，月在江樓倚玉簫。不用懷歸忘
　　　　此景，吳王看即奉弓招（陸龜蒙〈吳中即事〉）。
　　　　絕流而西，掠洇寺而過。寺在中流，重台傑閣，
　　　　方浮屠五層，輝映層波，亦澤國之一勝也（《徐
　　　　霞客遊記）。

　　翻譯成英文，印成小冊，正如上海太陽島島主陳逢坤老總所說，這項文化工程，也是太陽島五星級度假村國際化重要建設之一。但是翻譯工程複雜，先請新加坡國立大學的梁秉賦安排學生葉舒瑜與吳美玉做基礎翻譯，然後我與何蓮玉再作修改潤飾等工作，但是仍然不滿意。這只能當作試印本。

王潤華 / 陳逢坤　2010/5

1.For My Cousin Cheqi [1]

by Lu Ji (Jin Dynasty)

The lonely beast misses its previous shelter[2],
The birds sing a sorrowful tune when leaving the forest.
The carefree soul wandering afar,
Why is he always fretting?
This northern part of Lake Mao[3],
I dare say it is as mesmerizing as Mount Kun.
His heart is deeply concerned with his homeland,
His mood thus greatly affected by what he hears about his homeland.
He hardly sleeps well at night;
He seeks to speak out what is bothering his mind.
The return journey is so arduous,
I cannot help but begrudge my yearning.
It will be good to grow a grass called forget- to-go- home ,
Perhaps I should plant it by the northern side of my house.
My words may sound like a contrived argument,
Yet the solo bird longing for its partner is capable of driving one to tears.

Lu Ji (261-303) , courtesy name Shiheng, Western Jin dynasty poet and a native of Huating in present-day Songjiang of Shanghai. He lived north of Little Mount Kun. Lu wrote many poems and other works. He and his younger brother, Lu Yun are both known as "The Two Lus". His works are compiled in *The Collected Works of Lu Shiheng*. His "Essay on Literature" is an insightful study on the history of literature and art in China. Lu was also an accomplished calligrapher.

---

1 His brother Cheqi is also named Ye and Shi Guang. He had a good reputation from young. The poet Lu Ji claimed that he felt inferior when compared to Ye.
2 In the original poem, the words can mean a place for people to gather or a shelter for animals.
3 In the original poem, the words can be literally translated into "the northern side of the river in the valley"; "waters in the valley" refers to River Mao.

1　贈從兄車騎[4]

陸機（晉）

孤獸思故藪[5]，離鳥悲舊林
翩翩遊宦子，辛苦誰為心？
彷彿谷水陽[6]，婉孿昆山陰。
營魄懷茲土，精爽若飛沈。
寤寐靡安豫，願言思所欽。
感彼歸途艱，使我怨慕深。
安得忘歸草，言樹背與襟。
斯言豈虛作，思鳥有悲音。

　　陸機（261-303），字士衡。晉吳郡華亭（今上海松江）人，家住昆山（今小昆山）之北。西晉文學家。詩文甚富。與弟陸雲齊名，稱「二陸」。有《陸士衡傳》。所作《文賦》，為中國文學史和美學史上的一篇有創見的重要文章，其他如《演連珠》、《辨亡論》等，影響亦大。還擅長書法，流傳至今的《平復帖》，為中國現存最早的名人手跡（藏故宮博物館）。

　　本詩為《雲間志》所錄，僅有前面八句，尚缺八句，茲據晉《陸士衡傳》卷五補。又本詩入選梁蕭統《文選》卷二十四，可參閱。

4　從兄車騎 —— 名曄，字士光，事蹟見《晉書》卷七十七本傳。
　　傳說中他「少有雅望」，陸機每稱之曰：「我家世不乏公矣。」
5　故藪 —— 老窠。藪，人或物聚集的地方。
6　谷水陽 —— 泖河又稱谷水。谷水陽即指泖河的北面。

2.Poem on Wu Valley

by Lu Guimeng（Tang Dynasty）

On this antique land which nurtures the previous dynasties
with the refreshing wind,

It is never boring with the many anecdotes from the past.

The waves of River Mao alert the fishes and water plants；

Both the pheasants and the bait feel exhausted on the spring
grasses of the hunting ground.

The clouds conceal the monastery in the wild, and golden
pagoda is divided.

While the moon rises near the building beside the river,
someone is playing the jade flute.

There is no need to be too preoccupied with the thought of
returning home, you are unable to forget this beautiful
scenery.

The King of Wu will soon send the arrow of invitation.

Lu Guimeng （circa 881）, courtesy name "Luwang", Late Tang
dynasty poet and a native of Changzhou in present-day Suzhou.
He styled himself " Wanderer of the World", "He Who Follows
The Heaven", and "The Learned One of Fuli". Lu held official
positions in Suzhou and Huzhou. His works include *The
Collected Works of Fuli*.

2 吳中即事

陸龜蒙（唐）

風清地古帶前朝，遺事紛紛未寂寥。
三泖涼波魚蘢動，五茸春草雉媒嬌。
雲藏野寺分金剎，月在江樓倚玉簫。
不用懷歸忘此景，吳王看即奉弓招。

　　陸龜蒙（？-約 881），字魯望，自號江湖散人，天隨子，
甫里先生。長州（今江蘇蘇州）人。晚唐文學家。曾任蘇湖二
郡從事。著《耒耜經》及詩文集《甫里先生集》、《小名錄》、
《笠澤叢書》等。

　　本詩見《甫里先生集》。《雲間志》載：「三泖涼波魚蘢
動」一句，並註曰：「吾遠祖士衡對晉五帝。三泖冬溫夏涼蓋
謂此也。」

3.Mao River

by Song Yang（Song Dynasty）

The green ducks on the eastern slopes are lovely;

The fruits of clouds are planted on the western field.

Plowing this land the fish and birds roam freely,

unrolling the endless sceneries of the rivers and lakes.

At sunset, the moon is often reflected in the water by the shores,

Mist will form in the forest when the weather gets overly cold.

The gentleman would like to be a fisherman,

or as a wood cutter for many years.

Song Yang （996-1066）, first named as Jiao, with "Gongxu" as his courtesy name. A poet of the Song dynasty, he was a native of Anlu of Anzhou in present-day Hubei. He was conferred the title of *jingshi* （top scholar）, during the reign of Emperor Renzong of the Song dynasty. Song Yang held the concurrent posts of Premier and Deputy Minister of Defense. He was well-known for his essays and virtues, and specialized in the study of ancient Chinese scripts. His literary works are compiled in *The Collected Works of Song Yuanxian.*

3　三泖

宋庠（宋）

綠鴨東陂已可憐，更因雲實注西田。
鑿開魚鳥忘情地，展盡江湖極目天。
向夕舊灘多浸月，過寒薪樹便藏煙。
使君直欲稱漁叟，願賜樵青不計年。

宋庠（996-1066），初名郊，字公序，安州安陸（今湖北安陸）人。天聖初舉進士第一，官至兵部侍郎同平章事。早以文行負重名，晚年尤精字學。有《宋元憲集》、《國語補音》等。

本詩〈三泖〉指泖河，也稱泖湖，古有大泖、圓泖、長泖，即是今之泖河。古時圓泖中有一個小洲（即今太陽島），唐乾符年間（874-979）福田寺僧如海建築澄照禪院和五層浮屠。

4.The River in Huating Valley

by Tang Xun（Song Dynasty）

The River runs in the deep valley that stretches a thousand miles,

Joins Songling River in the north.

The water is almost as high as the river banks, blurring the contour of the field in the day;

People arrive and compete in a boat race.

When the moon shines, the local toad croaks;

The wind approaches the fragile floating water plants from the front.

The flat slope is infinitely far away,

Everywhere is filled with the refreshing autumn.

Tang Xun, courtesy name "Yanyou", Song dynasty poet and native of Qiantang in present-day Hangzhou.Tang Xun was conferred the title of *jingshi* （top scholar） during the reign of Emperor Renzong of the Song dynasty （1023-1031）. He was appointed as an official in charge of regulating remonstrance in the Board of Edicts. After receiving a piece of calligraphy written by Ouyang Xun, he was determined to master the art of calligraphy, and eventually carved a name for himself in this art form. His calligraphic strokes were beautiful, and he would not write without the best silk （paper?） and brush.

4 華亭谷

唐詢（宋）

深谷彌千里，松陵北合流。
岸平迷畫野，人至競方舟。
月照方諸泣，風迎弱荇浮。
平坡無限遠，極目漲清秋。

唐詢，字彥猷（墨池編作彥遊），錢塘（今杭州）人。天聖（1023-1031）中賜進士及第，累遷右諫議大夫。嘗得歐陽詢書數行，精思學之，遂以書名天下。筆跡遒媚，非精縑佳筆不妄書。

本詩見嘉慶刊《松江府志·名跡志》。古時有稱谷水、谷泖，此處所謂谷亦有指河之意。

5.The River in Huating Valley[1]

This poem is written to the tone of the seventh poem of
Tang Yanyou's "Ten Poems on Huating"

by Mei Yaochen（Song Dynasty）

This river cutting through Huating Valley is three hundred
miles long,
flowing into the Song River like a belt.
Although there is no utopia hidden by the river,
there are always fishing boats on the water.
In my leisure I see flying birds,
their many eyes are looking at the scattered wine cups and
tokens.
There is no need to ride on a whale[2] like Li Bai,
to be away for a few thousand years.

Mei Yaochen（1002-1060）, courtesy name "Shengyu", Northern
Song dynasty poet and native of Xuancheng in present-day Anhui.
He was conferred the title of *jingshi*（top scholar） after sitting
in the Imperial examination presided by the emperor, and held an
important position in the central government. Mei Yaochen's
works are found in *The Collected Works of Wanling*.

---

1 The original title literally means "Huating Valley", but it also
　refers to the river flowing in the valley. This river is also
　called "Three Mao".
2 Ride on a whale: Li Bai called himself "the one who rides a
　whale on the sea". It was rumored that he once rode on a whale
　while he was drunk. Du Fu wrote a line, "If I met Li Bai riding
　on a whale" in his poem.

5　華亭谷³依韻和唐彥猷華亭十詠

（之七）

梅堯臣（宋）

斷岸三百里，縈帶松江流，
深非桃花源，自有漁者舟。
閑意見飛鳥，目共汛舤籌。
何當騎鯨魚⁴，一去幾千秋。

梅堯臣（1002-1060），字聖俞，宣城（今安徽宣城）人，賜進士出身，官至尚書都官員外郎。北宋著名詩人，著有《宛陵先生文集》，又曾註釋《孫子》。

本詩見嘉慶刊《松江府志·名跡志》。

3　華亭谷 —— 即華亭縣內的谷水。又稱三泖。
4　騎鯨魚 —— 李白自署「海上騎鯨客」，俗傳他醉騎鯨魚。杜甫有「若逢李白騎鯨魚」詩句。

6.The River in Huating Valley

This poem is written to the tone of the eighth poem of Tang Yanyou's "Ten Poems on Huating"

by Wang Anshi

A big river does not have only one source.

It has tributaries in midstream.

Water in this valley is shallow.

Yet Song River[1] is able to make a boat capsize.

The fish and other water creatures do not know anything,

All they do is swim up and down the river.

I can only be astonished by the vastness of the river mouth,[2]

And the current is strong and flows eternally.

Wang Anshi （1021-1086）, Northern Song dynasty poet and politician, and native of Linchuan in present-day Fuzhou of Jiangxi. He annotated *The Book of Poetry*, *The Book of History* and *The Rites of Zhou*. His works include *The Collected Works of Wang Linchuan*, and *Supplements of the Collected Works of Wang Linchuan.*

---

1 "Song River" refers to Wusong River.
2 In the original poem, it was mentioned that the river mouthis located in present-day Daying Habour, north of Qingpu County. This is one of the five largest river mouths of Wusong River.

6　華亭谷次韻唐彥猷華亭十詠

（之八）

王安石（宋）

巨川非一源，源亦在中流。
此谷乃清淺，松江[3]能覆舟。
蟲魚何所知，上下相沉浮。
徒嗟大盈浦[4]，浩浩無春秋。

　　王安石（1021-1086），北宋傑出的政治家、文學家。字介甫，晚號半山，江西臨川（今江西撫州）人。曾註釋《詩經》、《尚書》、《周官》，著作今存《王臨川集》、《臨川集拾遺》等。

　　本詩在嘉慶刊《松江府志·名跡志》中題作《泖湖》。現據《臨川先生文集》卷十三校訂，以恢復原貌。

　　本詩見《臨川先生文集》卷十三。

---

3 松江 —— 即吳淞江。
4 大盈浦 —— 在青浦縣北面，現稱大盈港，爲吳淞江五大浦之一。

7.The Mao Pagoda

by Wang Feng（Yuan Dynasty）

When was this pagoda built and this extraordinary sight created?

It is as though it possesses the power of the water dragon, somersaulting while flying upwards.

The prisoner of Qin ends up in the land of the dead;

The treasure of Buddha calms the choppy water.

In this rainy night that needs several lamps to light up, I look at the scenery of the countryside;

The cold moon is like a mirror hanging in the dark sky.

I wish to buy a small boat so as to write a poem on the light of the fishing boat,

But I am too old and thus unable to visit the official-in-charge.

Wang Feng （1319-1388）, Yuan dynasty poet. He first moved to Suzhou to evade social unrest before settling down in Shanghai. Wang was adept at composing poetry and excelled in calligraphy. His publications include *The Collection of Wu Stream*, *The Original Meaning of Du Fu's Poetry*, and *Commentary on the Book of Poetry*.

7 泖塔

王逢（元）

何年窣堵聳奇觀，勢若蛟龍上鬥蟠。
秦縣赭衣淪鬼國，梵家寶藏壓驚湍。
野瞻雨黑重燈夜，天臥空青一鏡寒。
欲買扁舟占漁火，老緣無力候衡官。

王逢（1319-1388），字原吉，號梧溪子，最閑園丁，席帽山人，江陰人。避亂於淞，復徙上海。工詩，尤書。著《梧溪集》，撰輯《杜詩本義》、《詩經講說》二十卷等。

本詩見嘉慶刊《松江府志·名跡志》。

8.Mao River

by Qian Weishan

Grazing at the vast land in the west, the faraway sky is boundless.
And the nine peaks of Songjiang region[1] are full of grace.
The dragon's nest possesses power, tossing the waters upside down.
And its aura reaches as high as the moon and the stars of Dipper and Ox in the north.
High Monk Zhidun would visit this remote temple on every trip;
Guimeng also would keep his promise to plough and sow by the lake.
Before I can fully admire the scenery from above while leaning on the railings,
I board the boat which can travel ten thousand miles with the help of the wind.

Qian Weishan, Yuan dynasty poet. His hometown was Qiantang but he lived in Huating. He achieved fame for writing *The Rhapsody on Rakshasa* at the provincial examination. His literary piece, *The Collection of River, Moon, Pine and Wind,* had a limited circulation after it was published in the Late Ming dynasty. Prominent collectors obtained their copies by duplicating from the original manuscript.

---

1 The original words referring to the nine peaks of Songjiang region literally mean "nine water lilies". The beauty of women and peaks in poetry is commonly described by analogy with water lilies

8　泖湖

錢惟善（元）

西望滄茫浴遠天，芙蓉九點[2]秀娟娟。
勢翻震澤蛟龍窟，氣浸高寒牛鬥躔。
支遁每招過野寺，龜蒙曾約種湖田。
倚欄不盡登臨興，更駕長風萬里船。

　　錢惟善，錢塘人，定居華亭。早年鄉試以《羅剎賦》得名。著《江月松風集》，其集在明代末刻而傳稀，諸藏書名家據錢氏手稿本傳抄。

　　本詩見嘉慶刊《松江府志·山川志》。

2　芙蓉九點 —— 指松江九峰。詩歌中常用芙蓉（蓮荷）來比喻女子、山峰的美貌。

9. The River in Huating Valley

Written to the tone of Tang Yanyou's "Ten Poems on Huating Valley"

By Duan Tianyou （Yuan Dynasty）

The river in the valley stretches over three hundred miles,

And flows towards the east in this rainy night.

I raise my head and admire the trees on Mount Kun,

And row the boat on River Jiang.

Whitewaters appear with the waves;

The moon seems to be floating with the cloud.

Those who try to seek a position outside their home

Usually return home early in autumn for the perch[1].

Duan Tianyou's hometown was the city of Bian located in Kaifeng of Henan today. The highest position he held was the regulator of the learning of Confucianism in the Suzhou and Zhejiang region. He was famous for his calligraphy.

（The perch is a fish found in lakes and rivers so it is incorrect to translate it as "sea perch"）

---

1 The perch is a type of fish found only in Songjiang of Shanghai. It has a big head, a wide mouth and a flat stomach. As its meat is white and delicious, the perch is regarded as a delicacy.

9　華亭谷追和唐彥猷華亭十詠

段天佑（元）

谷水三百里，夜雨向東流。
仰瞻昆山樹，下泛松江舟。
白波兼浪起，素采與雲浮。
遊宦歸來蚤，鱸魚[2]正及秋。

　　段天佑，字吉甫，汴（今河南開封）人。官至江浙儒學提
舉。能書。

　　本詩見嘉慶刊《松江府志·山川志》。

2　鱸魚 —— 上海松江的特產。頭大嘴闊，腹部底平，肉質白而鮮美，
　　爲宴餐佳餚。

10.Mao River

by Zhang Yu（Yuan Dynasty）

There is a route linking Mao River to the Milky Way,
Thousands of miles filled with silver-flower ripples.
When will I be able to have a boat that is loaded with wine?
And on it carries a lady as beautiful as Xi Shi.

Zhang Yu, a poet lived through the Yuan and Ming dynasties and
he was also known as "The Laughing Recluse".

10　泖湖

張昱（元）

泖湖有路接天津，萬頃銀花小浪勻。
安得滿船都是酒，船中更載浣紗人。

張昱，字光弼。號一笑居士，廬陵人。跨元、明兩代詩人。
本詩見嘉慶刊《松江府志·山川志》。

11.Ascending Mao Pagoda

by He Liangjun（Ming Dynasty）

Ascending the pagoda which is standing in the middle of
Mao River,
I can see the nine peaks cozily surrounding the valley.
Its shoreline is spotted with countless tall trees,
Just the perfect backdrop by the gleaming waters;
On the river banks, the rushes and wild reeds[1],
Lend an alluring ambience to this whole scenery.

He Liangjun （1506-1573）, Ming Dynasty poet and native of.
Huating in present-day Songjiang of Shanghai. He excelled in
painting and poetry, and owned a huge library of books. Some of
the books written by him are *Collections from Four-Friends
Library*, *Appreciating Paintings and Poetry*, *Collections of Ho
Hanlin* and *Master Ho's Discourse*.

---

1 Reeds are a type of plants that grow in shallow water.

11 登泖詞

何良俊（明）

登泖上浮圖，見九峰環列，
　帶以長林，與波光相映，
　隔岸蒲葦[2]，點綴如染。

　　何良俊（1506-1573），字元朗，號柘湖居士，明華亭（今
上海松江）人。善畫山水，工詩文。著《四友齋叢說》、《書
畫銘心錄》、《何翰林集》、《何氏語林》等。藏書萬卷。
　　本詞見《青浦文物史話》。

---

2 蒲葦 —— 香蒲和蘆葦，草本植物，生長在淺水裡。

12.The Mao Lake

by Wang Shizhen

Do not complain that this lake is too small,
The vastness of water meets the sky at four corners.
The surface of the lake is as clear as a mirror,
The marsh grasses grow wild like fire.
The blue eyes of the eagle share the same color as this water,
The nine peaks are red not unlike the head of a condor.
Sounds of chanting are in harmony with the gentle ripples,
Songs of the fishermen can be heard amidst the chilly night.
It is easy to spread the teaching of Buddhism,
But it is difficult to uncover a mirage.
I am much too drunk,
Isn't it magical that I was served with these delicacies?
Taking a rest on my bed, I am a little tired,
Let me casually flip through a couple of the Buddhist texts.
One is still attached to many earthly desires,
I am ashamed of those who dare claim to know the Premier.

Wang Shizhen （1526-1590）, Ming dynasty poet and native of Taicang in Jiangsu. He was conferred the title of *jingshi* （top scholar） in 1547 and appointed Minister of the Board of Punishment in Nanjing in 1589. Although he was well-versed in calligraphy and painting, Wang was better known for his literary talents. His books include *Random Writings from the Yi Court* and *Four Works from Yan Zhou*.

12　泖湖

王世貞（明）

莫言初地小，但覺四天寬。

面面芙蓉鏡，層層薜荔冠。

一泓鶩眼碧，九點鬟頭丹。

唄響波聲合，漁歌夜色寒。

經歸龍藏易，僧結蜃樓難。

我醉聲聞酒，誰施法喜餐？

倦分禪榻臥，閑借佛書看。

猶有餘根在，羞人識宰官。

王世貞（1526-1590），字元美，號鳳洲，江蘇太倉人。嘉靖二十六年（1547）進士，萬曆十七年（1589）官至南京刑部尚書。善書兼善畫。以文學名。著《藝苑巵言》、《弇州四部稿》等。

本詩見嘉慶刊《松江府志·山川志》。

13. An Account of Sailing to Mao River in Autumn

by Mo Ruzhong（ Ming Dynasty）

Shortly afterwards, we reached the Mao River. Two monks came out from Pagoda Temple to greet us by shouting: "Are you fishermen?" After meeting us, they were surprised to say: "You are our rare guest. Did you have a difficult trip?" Then we were at ease and asked other friends to go ashore. Master Su led us into the hall where we were served tea. When we made a move, it started raining. The monks said: "Wait for a while, it is the end of the storm". A few minutes later, the rain and wind stopped. The evening sunshine came into the hall and the sky was bright. My heart was brightened and I took my friends to tour the courtyards, the new buildings and the pond for liberating live creatures. We also visited the meditation hall, the library of Buddhist sutras and books by many writers.

After climbing up the second storey of the pagoda, I looked around the scenic spots of Mao River and found everything within my view. The towns in the county covered by the clouds and mist were behind me. The nine peaks appeared in the distance as the famous mountains in Kusu were indistinctly visible. It is marvelous.

When I went to bed, I heard again the wind blowing violently and the waves roaring. It was more terrible than what happened before. I felt I was floating and the temple was flying in the air. After a while, a friend came in from outside and said: "The moon just appeared, don't miss it!" I open the window and saw that the sky outside was clear. There was a big moon so bright and shining, I could see the faces of my friend very clearly......

Mo Ru-zhong（ 1508-1588） was born in Huating, in present-day Songjiang of Shanghai. He was a noted calligrapher, poet and essayist.

13　秋日泛泖記

莫如忠（明）

宋。湖得曹平輒之：「余不望環，中諸，理異、潛與午蕩遂若、罷泖蘇晡名前至翳，然案各、拊頭興、不子龍卓簌，行袁而？會已新築覽姑且善視外劃見既歸馬，如昨為，而發境？影馮是。舟人中數渚門至步亦出二峰齋床怒一天乃顧之。加於奔勢如嗟夫之跡，為咎幾何，如昨為，而發境？

者子練，三浪飲牛門至步亦出二階離中坐怒友二峰齋床濤一返踞胡風間有營寥寥諸後諸友飯應半而勢如奔夫之跡，為咎幾何，坦途，必若此之為，哉？

余余如屬可巨鱄乎山險起風冒欲霽庭廡上九憩胡風間有營寥寥，諸後諸友漫半而勢如奔，嗟夫之跡，為咎幾何，如坦途，必若此之為，哉？

從而光益舟入引忡從冒欲霽庭廡作者篇翰咸返踞胡聞有複四可因宴具冊昨日風之一畫夜之外，日履坦途，必若此之

卿壁，水頃容出，喜節二已果曆遍諸友蹐微止飯寢飛上間而靄矣則動宇起宴具假昨風颯然西來，於是諸友謂余宜記其事，概斯遊於人生涉世

，從而光益舟入引僧奚之。」友經攜貯諸友攀盒觀友就如眉起宴具冊昨日風以片帆，縱一畫夜之外，日履坦途，必若此之

長侯流來之益赴院游茗頃遍及諸友蹐微止飯寢飛人射寢。僧已假昨風颯然西來，於是諸友謂余宜記其事，藉令委蜕所遭豈異哉，形骸所托，而斯遊當之，豈非幸

遊沈安而度上顧舷塔客啜。」諸友攀盒觀友就比樓閣西來禪林休焉，以莊生之喻大年，一畫夜之外，日履坦途，必若此之斑爾；

西、柵流逆至挽友扣水，「貴之風攜諸友念諸比樓起已西休焉，以莊生之喻大年，一畫夜之外，日履坦途，必若此之斑爾；

將宰鼓逆，力諸長：「入遺氤諸余氛諸辯，閣氤念，推戶視之，則芒成什也。僧已涼風颯林休焉，以莊生之喻大年，藉令委蜕所遭豈異哉，形骸所托，而斯遊當之，豈非幸哉？

余元，空舟子而聞俄長比氛念諸比辯，推戶視之，則宇眉起宴具册昨日風以片帆，縱一畫夜之外，日履坦途，造化過睱者之一斑爾；

，董朗撼漁漁，相及發閣先城而之辯，虛余郡，進甚虛人射寢。僧已涼風颯林休焉，以莊生之喻大年，一畫夜之外，日履坦途，豈非幸哉？

八甫日西覓從兩也則岸之餘精表背隱蒙，指見專難禦余記所不足者，誠得少涼風林休以莊生之喻大年，藉令委蜕所遭豈異哉，而斯遊當之，豈非幸

日、澄南兩，怖舟俄驚僧是乃閣。余郡，進甚虛人射寢。僧已涼風颯林休焉，以莊生之喻大年，藉令委蜕所遭豈異哉，而斯遊當之

有咸風從亞舟亦前，叩精表背隱蒙，如身發余記念所不足者，誠得少涼風林休焉，一畫夜之外，日履坦途，然後可語非常，而斯遊當之

十馮，風前因空在見登需户，還屠具最香為溫之日返生屠具最香光，而發余記念所未發，及福田禪而以莊生之喻大年，所遭奇跡，然後可語非常

，森，以沸之既友第叩霞截峩亦孰相如趣，照浮暄，生具香主之日返生屠具最香為溫之欲東，語口之興逆順殊於暗千古莊言，而還征以諸友之談空，又知凡昔所目睹，皆

秋幼氣衍泊，能趣：「及蔴相身，如生，在高積主之東，則諸念所未發，及福田禪感戚時奇跡，造化過睱者之一斑爾；然後可語非常，而斯遊當之

季君蕭泊，能琅趣曰：「及蔴相身，如負諸？」推戶視之，則余記念所未發，及興欣狀殊於暗千古莊言，而還征以諸友之談空，又知凡昔所目睹，皆

未蔡瀨移俱不聲知耶？」返照浮暄，放生屠具最香為溫之水飲漓欲東，語口之興逆順殊於暗千古莊言，而還征以諸友之談空，又知凡昔所

癸、水乃與余歌，漁撫，不舟然僧。然觀視勝山者甚曰：冰掌染盡則瞬余其眾之屢余事也；而餘言贅也。

陽發、橢以放遊「亦果烱堤仰諸名山僧者甚曰：冰掌染盡則瞬余其眾之屢余事也。

初晨口操攜地放遊「亦果烱堤仰諸勝山僧者甚曰：冰掌染盡則瞬余其眾之屢雅也；而餘言贅也。

莫如中（1508-1588），字子亮，化亭人（今上海市松江人）。嘉靖十七年（1538）近士。工書與詩文。有《崇蘭彼集》。本文見光緒刊《青浦縣誌》。

14.Sailing on the Mao River

By Mo Shilong（MingDynasty）

The lake illuminated by the moonlight seemed to sparkle at night,
When I emptied my wine, the sound of pine trees and waters could be heard.
I put on my coat to greet the guests,
As I call for wine, my voice wakes up the strong wind.
A flicker of the candlelight can be seen as the windows of the tall tower are pushed open.
The soft murmuring voice is up on the tower but their shadows are deep in water.
While the birds are chirping incessantly amidst swirling sand and the hazy gloom,
The monks in the ancient temple are concentrating on their meditation.
Many find their life akin to a drifting boat,
When would we realize that it was the same boat that manages to cut through the waves?
Among the nine peaks afar, one of them stood out distinctively,
Like a shiny white pearl that has once dazzled the Dragon Palace with its brilliance.
Climbing atop the mountain, this scenery is so vivid in my mind,
Its name gives me comforting warmth.
Even as the time passes by and I am no longer around,
This landscape will continue and endure like a miracle.

Mo Shilong （1537-1587）, Ming Dynasty poet and native of Huating in present-day Songjiang of Shanghai. Mo was an accomplished painter, poet and calligrapher. His works include *Collections from the Beautiful Stone Library*.

14 泛泖

莫是龍（明）

夜來湖上月色清，酒空惟聞松水聲。

使君攬衣起索客，呼酒長嘯天風生。

高樓推窗燭光冷，樓頭人語波心影。

沙磧煙荒鳥亂啼，陰廊古壁僧初定。

吾生茫茫都欲浮，何年擘浪分此印。

九龍峰前一珠耀，精芒直撼蛟宮溟。

登臨勝跡宛然在，姓字即令何曖曖。

欲待風流屠使君，千古江山起光怪。

　　莫是龍（1537-1587），字雲卿，號秋水，明華亭（今上海松江）人。工詩畫，善草書，喜散曲，精鑒賞、愛藏書。傳世作品有《淺絳山水圖》，書法作品《草書五律詩》，著有《石秀齋集》等。

　　本詩見嘉慶刊《松江府志·山川志》。

15.On Lake Mao

By Dong Qichang（Ming Dynasty）

Deep within the thick foliage, the nine peaks are lotus flowers.

The low-lying river reaches are like a palm, reflecting the autumn light.

Living in seclusion, the river seems longer,

Hidden in this remote region, it has become the lord of the valley.

When the sun sets, the fish find its way back to the gorges,

Soft chimes can be heard across the lake in this wintry evening.

What has one not seen in his arduous life?

Except such beauty that lies behind the reeds growing at Lake Mao.

Dong Qichang （1555-1636）, Ming Dynasty poet and native of Huating in present-day Songjiang of Shanghai, he was appointed Minister of the Board of Rites in Nanjing in 1625. Dong was an accomplished painter and poet, and a respected critic of these two art forms. As an artist, he enjoyed high esteem and played a leading role in shaping the philosophy of the Songjiang school of painting. His works include *The Rong Jie Collections*, *A Study of the Academic Discipline*, *Poems from the Four Prints Hall*, and *Anecdotes of the Nanjing Han Lin Academy*.

15 泛泖

董其昌（明）

九點芙蓉墮森茫，平川如掌攬秋光。

人從隱後稱湖長，水在封中表谷王。

日落魚龍回夜壑，霜清鐘聲隔寒塘。

浮生已閱風波險，欲問蒹葭此一方。

董其昌（1555-1636），字玄宰，號思白，別號香光居士。明華亭（今上海松江）人。天啓五年（1625），官至南京禮部尚書。生平以書畫及鑒賞知名。爲松江畫派首領，享譽藝壇。著作有《容介集》、《學科考略》、《四印堂詩稿》、《南京翰林院志》等。

本詩見嘉慶刊《松江府志・山川志》。

16.Crossing the Mao River

by Chen Jiru

I
The floating duckweeds set sail in the late autumn evening,
Whilst the rustling maple leaves decorate the sky with a red
hue.
One hardly expects such autumn serenity of Lake Mao,
To find its home behind the reeds that grows by this temple.

II
Imagine the swirling sand sediments beneath the calm
waters of Lake Mao,
The tall reeds seem to have concealed the broken bridge and
the entrance to the temple.
I wish I could borrow the strength from the wind,
Soaring above the lake like the sea gulls, sending waves
across the water.

III
The sun is setting in the west,
Yet this scenery is still an alluring sight as I proceed up the
stairs.
Looking out from the window, the overgrown vegetation
lends its lush to the entire place.
The flight of a pair of gulls greet the fisherman on his
home-coming journey.

Chen Jiru(1558-1639), Ming Dynasty poet and native of Huating
in present-day Songjiang of Shanghai. He called himself "The
Woodcutter living in White Stone Mountain". He was as famous
as the poet Dong Qichang who came from the same hometown. He
distinguished himself in painting and poetry, and owned a huge
collection of books. His works include *The Complete Collection
of Chen Mei Gong*. He was also the chief editor of *Poetry from
the Past and Present*.

16 渡泖

陳繼儒（明）

秋老江蘋漾夕空，蕭蕭楓葉掛疏紅。
那知三泖清秋思，偏寄蘆花一寺中。

泖上定波疊亂沙，寺門橋斷半蒹葭。
何從一借風帆力，醉挾飛鷗拍浪花。

斜陽約略水西頭，餘景還能上竹樓。
無際靡蕪半窗綠，釣蓑歸處起雙鷗。

　　陳繼儒（1558-1639），字仲醇，號眉公，又號白石山樵，華亭（今上海松江）人。與同郡董其昌齊名。工詩文，書畫。藏書頗豐。著作有《陳眉公全集》傳世，輯有《古今詩話》等，主纂《崇禎松江府志》。

　　本詩見嘉慶刊《松江府志・山川志》。

17.Pagoda Garden of Fu Tian Temple

by Tu Long（Ming Dynasty）

I climbed up Mao Pagoda and sat in the Buddhist scripture library. As I leaned against the railings and looked out, I was surrounded by mist and water. The giant pagoda was standing tall, amidst the smoke, clouds and lushness of green. The soaring surf was shaking the world day and night down below. The fish in the river, the birds on the sandbank, lotus flowers and the water-chestnut were living differently but in peace. The low and chilly sound of the temple bell was a response to the roaring of waves. Shortly afterwards, the broken rainbow was winding around and then was hanging itself on the branches of the trees.　The air with splendor and colorful clouds were fully reflected in the waves, and the temple buildings were flashing with gold. Then the moon appeared from the northern mountain peaks and the water was quiet as a mirror. The shining moon lights on the river created the golden image of Buddhist monetary. I felt drunk. Happily, my friends and I composed poetry and wrote journals. This is really a well-hidden, empty and quiet place, far away from the human world. It is an ideal place for seeking a life of self-exile or as a recluse. It is also the best place for a poet to be inspired among the clouds, mountains and rivers.

Tu Long （1542-1605）, native of Yinxian, a county in modern Zejiang province. He was conferred the *jinshi* （top scholar） in the fifth year of the Wanli period in the Ming dynasty. As the magistrate of Qingpu county, where Mao River and Mao Pagoda are sited, he was fond of inviting poets and officials to drinking and poetry sessions after cruising on the Mao River.

17　福田寺塔園記

屠隆（明）

登泖塔，坐藏經閣，憑欄瞻眺，四面煙水迴絕。大士浮圖，巍然矗立煙雲空翠間，洪濤衝擊，日夜撼其下。川魚沙鳥，芙蕖菱茨，參差曆落，鐘聲之音泠泠然，與波浪相答。少頃，斷虹蜿蜒，斜掛木杪，日氣霞彩，下射波心，殿閣回映閃爍，陡作黃金相。頃之，月出東嶺，波平如鏡，流光蕩漾，直是浮金剎舍，心灑焉，樂之。時與諸君各賦詩記遊，蓋幽峭空曠，離絕塵世，足資高流棲遁，詞人登覽，泖雲間山川。最勝處也。

屠隆（1542-1605），字長卿、緯真，號赤水，鴻苞居士。原籍浙江鄞縣，明萬曆五年進士。官青浦知縣。時招名士飲酒賦詩，縱遊九峰三泖而不廢吏文。有《鴻》、《考盤餘事》、《遊編》、《由拳集》、《白榆集》、《采真集》、《南遊集》等，又有傳奇劇《曇花記》、《修文記》、《彩豪記》三種。

本詩見嘉慶刊《松江府志·名跡志》。

18.Lake Mao

by Chen Cong（Ming Dynasty）

The trees with bare branches stood by the lake in the
autumn,
While the fishes swim leisurely amidst the chilling wind.
The gentle swooshing of the tides can be heard across the
deep valley,
And the pagoda seems to rise into the tall and misty skies.
A pavilion is found within the thick woods,
Its beauty lies not in what is being told by others.
At high tide, the blue mountain ranges are becoming black,
Nine lotus flowers are blooming beyond the horizon.

Chen Cong （1573-1620）, Ming dynasty poet, and native of
Wujiang in present-day Jiangsu. He was highly respected in his
village. Chen was a master poet, calligrapher and seal carver.

18　泖上

陳琮（明）

泖上秋來木落疏，涼風颯颯起龍魚。
潮音動地通長轂，塔勢連雲入太虛。
柴辟有亭傳越絕，由拳無縣紀秦餘。
來潮一望峰如黛，九朵芙蓉畫不如。

　　陳琮（1573-1620），鄉間名家。字叔正，一作正叔，吳江
（今江蘇吳江）人。能詩，書法遒美，兼工篆刻。

　　本詩見《青浦續詩傳（卷六）》。

19.Crossing the Mao River at night

by Zhang Chengxian（Ming Dynasty）

Carrying my bottles of wine and rowing my boat into the hazy gloom,

The sun is already setting, casting its dark shadow on the river and bridges.

The rising high tide seems to be churning out tons of snow,

Watch how the nimble white herons would cross this layer of frost.

All around, the moonlight engulfs the lake in its brilliance,

The lonely silhouette of a pagoda hovers over the lake.

I wonder if I have arrived in the magical realm.

Amidst the night breeze, I stand drinking and thinking about my family.

Zhang Chengxian, Ming dynasty poet. His hometown was Huating-in present-day Songjiang of Shanghai, but he lived in the town of Zhujing. Zheng was conferred the title of *jingshi* （top scholar） in the 23rd year of the Jiajing reign. His works include *Collections from Rui Liang Hall*.

19 月夜遊泖湖

張承憲（明）

載酒浮槎入混茫，荒荒落日滿河梁。

洪濤忽湧空中雪，白鷺遙翻水上霜。

四望波光涵灝月，獨懸塔影照滄浪。

恍疑身入蓬瀛境，把盞臨風思欲狂。

　　張承憲，字監先，華亭（今上海松江）人，居朱涇。嘉靖二十三年進士，著有《端諒堂集》。

　　本詩見《松江縣誌·卷二十六》。

20.Passing by the Mao River

Shen Mingchen（Ming Dynasty）

Passing by the Mao River one late autumn,

I saw fisherman shacks and fishing nets everywhere.

An empty hut stood plainly beside the towering tree,

Gentle ripples seem to reverberate in the cooling night

breeze.

Shen Mingchen, Ming dynasty poet and native of Yin County in present-day Ningbo of Zhejiang. He was a student of the Court Academician and talented in calligraphy. An active poet **of** the Jiajing reign, he composed no less than 7000 poems in his lifetime and was highly respected by his contemporaries.

20 泖上

沈明臣（明）

深秋泖上一經過，蟹舍魚罾處處多。
野屋無煙空綠樹，夜風天半響寒波。

沈明臣，字嘉則，鄞縣（今浙江寧波）人。爲博士弟子，善書。明代嘉靖時詩人，一生寫了七千多首詩，在當時很有詩名。

本詩見《松江縣誌·卷二十六》。

∠1.The Travelogue of Xu Xiake

by Xu Xiake（Ming Dynasty）

By early morning, Duke Mei had written a letter to introduce me to the two monks. He also invited me to stay for breakfast. I only started my journey in late morning. My previous journey was to the east, and now I travelled to the west. I passed by Mount Ren, after travelling for three miles, and Mount Tianma after travelling for three miles in the northwest direction. For another three miles in the west, I passed by Mount Heng. Yet another further two miles in the same direction, I passed by Little Mount Kun. With another three miles towards the west, I entered Mao River. After crossing the river and travelling towards the west, I passed by Mao Temple. The Temple is erected in the middle of the river. Among other magnificent temples and pavilions, there is a five-storey tall pagoda which is reflected in the waves of the river. The temple and the pagoda have become one of the most wonderful sights in this land of water. Upon reaching Qingan Bridge and travelling for ten miles, there is Zhanglian Pond which is located in the southern region of Changzhou where ten thousand families are living. Another ten miles to the west, there is Bay of the Jiang Family in Jiashan County. I chose to postpone my journey so as to wait for the numerous crab-catching boats to set out. I docked my boat at the house of the Ding Family （situated thirty-six miles north of Jiashan County, the homeland of High Official Duke Gaiting） without delay.

Xu Hongzu （1586-1641）, Ming dynasty writer and native of Jiagnyin in present-day Jiangsu, He was also known as "The Honorable Rosy Cloud". As a traveler and geographer since the age of 22, he travelled for over 30 years to various provinces. From his arduous journeys, he wrote the masterpiece, *The Travelogue of Xu Xiake,* This account is extracted from Volume Two of *Diary of My Tour in Zhejiang.* It recorded anecdotes about the people the author met while touring Qingpu and Mount She, and the changes happening in the region. In addition, his account of the Mao Temple Mao is especially intriguing because it arouses a sense of antiquity in the reader.

21　徐霞客遊記

（一則）

徐宏祖（明）

丙子[1]二十五日。清晨，眉公已為余作二僧書，且修以儀。復留早膳，為書王忠紉乃堂壽詩二紙，又以紅香米寫經大士饋余。上午始行。蓋前猶東遷之道，而至是為西行之始也。三里過仁山。有西北三里，過天馬山。又西三里，過橫山。又西二里，過小昆山。又西三里，入泖河。絕流而西，掠泖寺而過。寺在中流，重台傑閣，方浮屠五層，輝映層波，亦澤國之一勝也。西入慶安橋，十里，為章練塘（其地為長洲南境，亦萬家之市也）。又西十里，為蔣家灣，已屬嘉善。貪晚行，為聽蟹群舟所驚，亟入丁家宅而泊（任嘉善北三十六里，即尚書改亭公之故里）。

徐宏祖（1586-1641），字振之，號霞客。明南直隸江陰（今屬江蘇）人，旅行家，地理學家。不樂仕進。從二十二歲起曆三十多年，遍遊諸省，途中備嘗艱險，最後將其考察所得，寫成極有價值的《徐霞客遊記》。這裡所選二日日記，系卷二《浙遊日記》上途中在青浦、佘山所遇人情交往，世事變遷，頗饒興趣。對泖寺建築的讚美，更能令人發思古之幽情。

---

1 丙子（1636年，即明崇禎九年）。

22.Looking at the Nine Peaks from Mao River

by Zhang Qishi (Ming Dynasty)

Arriving in the south where the waters seem to join the skies,

Light winds are brushing against the shore, sending ripples across the lake.

The misty Nine Peaks are now clearly in sight,

Many layers of the smoke-covered forest are painted with a splash of green.

The songs of the fishermen can be vaguely heard in the midst of clouds,

The lonely silhouette of a pagoda gets reflected on the mirror-like surface of the lake.

I cannot wait to taste the water plant *chun* and perch fish from my hometown again,

But I must first fulfill my duties so as not to disappoint the sages.

Zhang Qishi, Ming dynasty poet and native of Huating present-day Songjiang of Shanghai. He distinguished himself in poetry and calligraphy.

22　泛泖遙望九峰

張其淵（明）

南來澤國水連天，夾岸風微瀉碧漣。
九點煙巒晴歷歷，數重煙樹晝芊芊。
漁歌縹渺雲中度，塔影孤清鏡裡懸。
為憶蓴鱸歸計早，臨流差不愧前賢。

張其淵，字季琰，華亭（今上海松江）人。善詩，書。
本詩見《松江縣誌·卷二十六》。

23.Climbing Up Mao Pagoda

Xu Xiangpo（Qing Dynasty）

The pagoda is standing in the middle of the River,

The water flowing in the four directions is like a mirror.

The rocks on the sand banks are bright.

The clouds under water are shining.

The cool wind of autumn arrives with a pair of cranes

The sudden rain at night takes the river dragons by surprise[1].

Leaning against the rail, I gaze serenely afar.

Soft chimes from the temple[2] can be heard over the skies.

Xu Xiangpo, Qing dynasty poet and native of Qingpu who lived in Xiaozhen by Lake Ling. Nicknamed "The Farmer by the Marsh", Xu was recognized as a talent in literature.

---

1 In the original poem, the words can be literally translated as making a sound or a hiss so as to startle the river dragons.
2 In the original poem, the words can be literally translated as the sound of the bells ringing in the temple.

23　登泖塔

徐蒒坡（清）

中流一塔湧，四面鏡奩分；
齒齒沙間石，鱗鱗水底雲；
秋風招鶴侶，夜雨嘯龍君[3]；
倚欄舒清眺，鐸鈴[4]天際聞。

徐蒒坡，字舊林，號澤農，青浦人，居小蒸菱塘灣。貢生，乾隆三十年南巡，召試得第二名。能文。

本詩見《青浦文物史話》。

3　嘯龍君 —— 驚動了龍君。
4　鐸鈴 —— 寺廟的鐘聲。

24.After Visiting Mao Pagoda

By Zhang Jiaqiu（Qing Dynasty）

It is best to climb the mountains on this clear day,
On my lonely boat I look far ahead, longing for home.
Amidst falling leaves and the homecoming crows,
My fishing boat in the autumn river is about to sail again..
The moon casts the shadow of the pagoda into the quiet courtyard.
Waters seem to rumble like thunder in the quiet night.
I plan to visit the Master tomorrow,
His mountain pavilion is near Heaven.

Zhang Jiaqiu, Qing dynasty poet and native of Zhangyan in Qingpu. He was also known as " Rosy Cloud of the West". Zhang's works include *Collections of Poems from Jin Mei.*

24　遊泖塔次日抵昆山訪旅庵大師

章駕秋（清）

晴日登臨好，孤舟遠眺回；
晚鴉楓葉落，秋水釣船開。
塔影閒庭月，濤聲靜夜雷；
來朝訪高衲，山閣近蓬萊。

章駕秋，字彥生，號西霞，為青浦章堰人。著《金湄詩草》。
本詩見《青浦續詩傳（卷一）》。

25.Climbing Up Mao Pagoda

By Zhu Weixing（Qing Dynasty）

A wooden raft is riding on the waves;

Casting its shadows, the pagoda seems to cut apart the flowing water.

The faraway river bank is cool because the moon is deep in the water.

The clouds are secretly hidden inside the old pagoda.1

I try to drink and recite poetry throughout the night2,

And reside by this peaceful lake as a recluse3.

Looking afar, I lean against the rail,

Sounds of chanting can be heard clearly across the sky.

Zhu Weixing, Qing dynasty poet and native of Qingpu. He was recommended to enroll in the State's highest education institution of his time as a *gongshen* （Imperial examination candidate）. He was acclaimed for his poetry.

---

1 In the original poem, the words "ancient monastery" can also mean "pagoda" during the Six Dynasty, After the Tang dynasty, they refer to " temple."

2 It is believed that the Ming literati Tu Chi Long once invited his friends to drink and recite poetry throughout the night on Lake Mao. Tu was from Qingpu, the same hometown as the poet Zhu Wei Xing.

3 It is believed that the poet Yang Qiu Ya built his hut by the Mao Lake and calls it better than heaven.

25 登泖塔

朱位行（清）

竹筏乘潮去，中流塔影分；
遙汀涼浸月，古刹[4]暗藏雲；
嘯詠追仙令[5]，棲遲羨隱君[6]；
危闌一憑眺，清梵半天聞。

朱位行，字因在，青浦人，拔貢生。能詩文。
本詩見《青浦文物史話》。

---

4 古刹 —— 六朝人稱塔曰刹，唐以後統稱佛寺曰刹。
5 嘯詠追仙令 —— 屠赤水官青浦時，曾與諸名士泛舟三泖，嘯詠終日。
6 棲遲羨隱君 —— 楊秋崖在泖湖建有草之閣，小蓬壺諸勝。

26.Crossing the Mao River

By Ye Jin (Qing Dynasty)

A lonely boat greets the setting sun,

Everywhere seems to be besieged by the blue sky.

The moon rises above the deep waters,

While the flight of wild geese cuts through the skyline.

Shrouded in dusk, the mountains look very far away,

The wanderer's thoughts venture further, along with the waves of the river.

They tell me that the Green Town is near,

The remote lake is covered by trees and smoke..

Ye Jing, Qing dynasty poet and native of the Nanxiang town of Jiading. A master engraver, he started composing poems at the age of 8 but was never successful in the imperial examinations. Ye was a reticent man who enjoyed reading. His goal was to edit the *History of Ming* as he felt that the account was incomplete. After he passed away, Ye's wife feared that his writings might invite trouble from the authorities and hence destroyed most of them.

26 渡泖

葉錦（清）

孤舟迎夕照，入望總蒼茫。
月上潮三尺，天空雁一行。
暮山隨意遠，客思與波長。
指點茸城近，村煙滿野塘。

　　葉錦，字魏堂，又字芳蓁，嘉定南翔鎮人。善刻印，有澄
懷堂印證。八歲能詩，試輒不利，至死不得一衿，生平寡言笑
好披閱古書當作明史補傳。歿後其妻恐有違礙悉焚之。著有馥
村詩二卷。摘自《青浦續詩傳》。
　　本詩見《松江縣誌・卷二十六》。

27.Written for the Painting "Sailing on River Mao in Autumn"

Jiang Jiapeng（Qing Dynasty）

Calm waves and light breeze paint a serene mood;

Shadows of the pagoda cast by the moonlight dance softly on the lake.

You are a man with foreboding ability,

Who produces a painting of Shao Bo and Yuan Ming.

The village is surrounded with clouds and waters,

And I sat afloat on my raft, reciting endless autumn poems.

Peace abound, not unlike the heart of the Buddha,

My little boat is a barge of compassion of the Goddess of Mercy

Jiang Jiapeng, Qing dynasty poet and native of Shanghai. Highly respected by many, he believed in the goodness of human nature and shared his wisdom widely on improving oneself and becoming successful. This poem was composed in the autumn of 1842.

27 題〈泖湖秋泛圖〉

江駕鵬（清）

浪靜風恬氣亦恬，月扶塔影貼波尖。
先生早有先機識，少伯淵明一幅畫。
煙波渺渺水雲鄉，泛棹吟秋興味長。
身似婆提心自在，飄然小艇即慈航。

　　江駕鵬，字翼雲，上海人，諸生。性好善，所著格言以濟
人利物為務，時稱長者。

28. Written for the Painting "Sailing on the Mao River in Autumn"

Zhou Jingyi（Qing Dynasty）

I travelled along the Mao River three times in the past,
But I I missed the opportunity to explore the scenery.
The shoreline is like an endless piece of white silk,
And above the waters, the moon lights the pathway with its softness.
My good friend Mr Zi Tian ,
Is living in the quiet woods covered by clouds.
The maple trees surrounding the river sands are hidden in mist,
And wilting reeds along the banks are shaking in the wind.
Deep within the reeds grew white flowers which resemble snowflakes;
Crystal clear sounds of chimes and waves can be heard across the lake in this cool autumn.
I know my friend is an outstanding soul,
Nonetheless he seeks the solace of a hidden life.
The vines circling his home render it hardly visible from sight,
But everyone is hesitating to leave even if the oars are ready.
For departure means a long farewell to this awesome landscape,
And a sense of loss akin to that of a fish caught, knowing that it will never ever return to the pond again.
Looking at the paintings, how I yearn for the taste of my hometown food;
I wish I could live in retreat like Yang Zhong and Qiu Zhong.

Zhou Jingyi, Qing dynasty poet and native of Huating in present-day Songjiang of Shanghai today. He was recommended to enroll in the State's highest education institution of his time as a *gongshen* （Imperial examination candidate） in 1837. This poem was composed in 1842.

28 題〈泖湖秋泛圖〉

周景頤（清）

昔年屢放三泖棹，惜未竟作三泖遊。
練塘白練望不極，申江弄月情彌遒。
惟我良友子恬子，家居益覺雲林幽。
紫楓繞灘煙漠漠，枯蘆夾岸風修修。
蒹葭深處花似雪，潮音鐘梵來清秋。
知君生平本超卓，逸思往往懷盟鷗。
數椽老屋互隱見，一枝柔櫓誰夷猶。
江山大地成久別，耿耿有若魚懸鉤。
披圖恍動蒪鱸憶，便擬結侶如羊求。

周景頤，字竹溪。道光十七年（1837）華亭（今松江）拔
貢生。

29. Written for the Painting "Sailing on the Mao River in Autumn"

By Lei Baolian (Qing Dynasty)

Returning to the Mao River on a lonely boat,

I am wandering deep in the cluster of reeds.

A pagoda is standing up still and tall, almost touching the skies;

The noise of the rising tide is thundering in my ears.

Chimes can be heard from afar, probably behind the dense clouds;

The peaks shaped like nine lotus flowers are blooming in the distance.

Cutting through the woods, the pathway leading from the pavilion is an endless route;

This whole place is shrouded in a peaceful yet dreamy atmosphere.

Lei Baolian, Qing dynasty, also known as "Founder of Hua Pavilion Lotus Society". This poem was composed in the autumn of 1843.

29 題〈泖湖秋泛圖〉

雷葆廉（清）

載得孤舟泖上回，荻蘆深處一徘徊；
摩空塔勢連雲起，到耳潮音動地來。
鐘盤幾聲雲外落，芙蓉九朵望中開；
迢迢柴辟亭前路，煙水溟蒙絕點埃。

雷葆廉，字蓮隱，華亭蓮社主人。

30. Written for the Painting "Sailing on the Mao River in Autumn"

By Yuan Kejia (Qing Dynasy)

Low-lying clouds have blocked the tracks leading to the river,

The autumn leaves above the water have turned red.

Do not try to bribe me with a thousand bottles of wine or a million scrolls of books,

Just send me to this lovely village by the lakeside.

Yuan Kejia, Qing dynasty poet. He called himself "the man who is never bothered by small things". This poem was composed in the summer of 1844.

30 題〈泖湖秋泛圖〉

袁克家（清）

白雲低鎖湖邊路，紅葉斜開水上門；
酒一千瓶書萬卷，只應抬我住江村。

袁克家，自稱小事糊塗。

國家圖書館出版品預行編目資料

上海太陽島詩選 / 王潤華,陳逢坤編選. -- 初
版. --臺北市：文史哲，民 99.07
面： 公分. -- （文史哲詩叢；91）
ISBN 978-957-549-906-8(平裝)

851.486　　　　　　　　　　99010123

文史哲詩叢　91

上海太陽島詩選

編選者：王　潤　華・陳　逢　坤
出版者：文　史　哲　出　版　社
http://www.lapen.com.tw
登記證字號：行政院新聞局版臺業字五三三七號
發行人：彭　　　正　　　雄
發行所：文　史　哲　出　版　社
印刷者：文　史　哲　出　版　社
臺北市羅斯福路一段七十二巷四號
郵政劃撥帳號：一六一八○一七五
電話886-2-23511028・傳真886-2-23965656

實價新臺幣一四○元

中華民國九十九年（2010）七月初版